Hugs

x

ELLA EARLE

summersdale

HUGS

Images © Shutterstock

With research by Alistair Cruickshank and Chloe Hughes

Summersdale Publishers Ltd
46 West Street
Chichester
West Sussex
PO19 1RP
UK

www.summersdale.com

Printed and bound in China

ISBN: 978-1-84953-680-6

Substantial discounts on bulk quantities of Summersdale books are available to corporations, professional associations and other organisations. For details contact Nicky Douglas by telephone: +44 (0) 1243 756902, fax: +44 (0) 1243 786300 or email: nicky@summersdale.com.

To...

From..

A hug is the perfect gift – one size fits all and nobody minds if you exchange it.

IRVIN BALL

*The best thing
to hold on to in life
is each other.*

AUDREY HEPBURN

Hugs...

are the best way to share love.

*The language of
friendship is not
words but meanings.*

HENRY DAVID THOREAU

Happiness is an unexpected hug.

ANONYMOUS

You can *never* run out of hugs.

They invented hugs to let people know you love them without saying anything.

BIL KEANE

A hug means
more than
words
can say.

A moment shared between
two doubles the
happiness.

You can't wrap love in a box, but you can wrap a person in a hug.

ANONYMOUS

Love is a circular emotion that surrounds you, like a hug.

Jarod Kintz

True friends...

will always be there
when you need them.

*I love hugging. I wish
I was an octopus,
so I could hug ten
people at a time.*

DREW BARRYMORE

Nothing

warms you up
faster than a hug.

A hug is the *perfect* way to express friendship.

There is nothing better than a friend, unless it is a friend with chocolate.

LINDA GRAYSON

Everyone needs to hug and be...

hugged.

Laughing together is as close as you can get to a hug without touching.

GINA BARRECA

*People… who love you…
put their arms around
you and love you when
you're not so lovable.*

DEB CALETTI

The best hugs are
spontaneous.

I think that beauty comes from being happy and connected to the people we love.

MARCIA CROSS

I hug you just

because

I can.

True friends bring
a burst of

sunshine

into life.

My best friend is the one who brings out the best in me.

HENRY FORD

Friends

laugh and cry
with you.

Hugs can do great amounts of good.

Great friends will
happily spend hours
in each other's
company.

Hugs are *always* the right size.

I have learned that there is more power in a good strong hug than in a thousand meaningful words.

ANN HOOD

Life is better
when it's
shared
among friends.

There's
nothing
like a hug
to get you through
the day.

Friendship is a sheltering tree.

SAMUEL TAYLOR COLERIDGE

*Love... it surrounds
every being and extends
slowly to embrace
all that shall be.*

Kahlil Gibran

A hug is a *universal* sign of friendship.

The friend who holds your hand and says the wrong thing is... dearer... than the one who stays away.

BARBARA KINGSOLVER

Be slow to fall into friendship; but when thou art in, continue firm and constant.

SOCRATES

A hug is
the best
medicine.

*A hug is a handshake
from the heart.*

ANONYMOUS

Friends are
the ones who
love you
just the way
you are.

A hug is a gift you
give and

receive

at the same time.

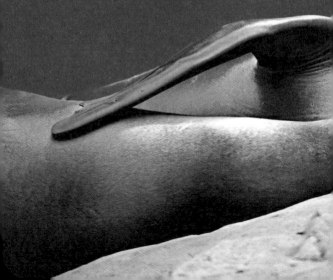

Being with you
makes me
relax.

Nuptial love maketh mankind; friendly love perfecteth it.

FRANCIS BACON

*The love we
give away is the
only love we keep.*

ELBERT HUBBARD

A hug is free
therapy.

Hugs make
everything
better.

Friends are the family you choose.

JESS C. SCOTT

*We need four hugs
a day for survival…
eight hugs a day for
maintenance… twelve
hugs a day for growth.*

VIRGINIA SATIR

A hug is a universally accepted method of...

affection.

A hug is like a boomerang – you get it back right away.

BIL KEANE

Hugs are an easy way
to show someone
you care.

There is nothing on this earth more to be prized than true friendship.

THOMAS AQUINAS

A hug lasts
long after
you let go.

x x

A hug
from you
brightens
up a gloomy day.

Love is the oil that eases friction, the cement that binds closer together, and the music that brings harmony.

EVA BURROWS

A hug overcomes all boundaries. It speaks words within the mind that cannot be spoken.

ANONYMOUS

You
always
make me smile.

*Forever friends are
a treasure chest
of understanding
and compassion.
Cherish them.*

AMY LEIGH MERCREE

The best hugs
are from the
heart.

Recycle kisses, hugs and smiles; they never go out of style and everybody needs one.

CRYSTAL DeLARM CLYMER

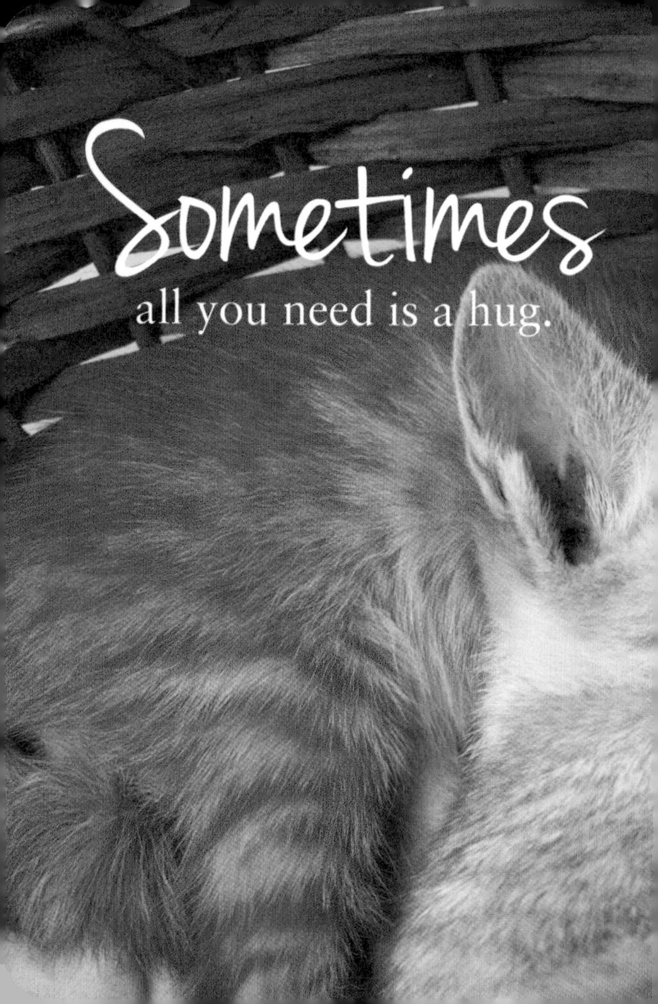
Sometimes
all you need is a hug.

Give someone an
unexpected
hug today.

If you're interested in finding out more about our books, find us on Facebook at

Summersdale Publishers

and follow us on Twitter at

@Summersdale.

www.summersdale.com